D0539507

Hi, I'm Chris.

Right now, I'm feeling fed up.

I never get to choose anything myself.

My mum, my dad and my sister Kate all choose things they like.

Me?

Never!

1

Take last night.

Mum was back late from work.

"Shall we have a take-away?" she asked.

"What shall we get?"

"PIZZA!" shouted Kate.

"Is that OK with you, Chris?" Mum said.

"Yeah, yeah! Whatever you like," I said.

Why do we always have pizza?
Why can't we have Chinese for
a change?

3

On Tuesday it was the same.

I wanted to watch Man United play Arsenal on BBC1.

"There's a nature programme on ITV after *EastEnders*," said my dad. "Does anyone mind if I watch it?"

"Go ahead," I said. "Don't mind me."

It's the same with clothes, too.

Last Saturday my mum said I needed
a new pair of shoes.

We went into town.

Mum spotted a pair in the shoe shop
window.

"Those leather ones look just right," she
said, "and they're very good value. Shall
we try them on?"

I tried them on, and Mum paid for them.

Why can't I have some trainers, like
my friends?

And another thing!

Whenever we go out in the car, Kate chooses what we listen to.

It's always local radio. It's really naff!

She always gets in there first.

Why can't I play one of my CDs?

This morning we're going to town.
Mum says I need a haircut.

Is your mum like this?

Mum comes into the hairdresser's with me.
It's so embarrassing!

"What would you like me to do?" asks the
hairdresser.
"What do you think, Chris?" my mum says.
"Just a tidy up?"
"OK, OK. Fine." I say.
"I've got some shopping to do," she says.
"I'll be back as soon as I can. Wait for
me," she says.
Then she leaves.

She's always choosing things for me.

"Are you OK with a 'tidy up'?" the hairdresser asks.

"Can I have something different?"

"Sure," says the hairdresser. "Do you know what you want?" I point to a photo on the wall.

"Can I have something like that?" I ask.

"Why not?" she says. "Be a devil!"

Well, I've done it.

I've chosen something for myself.

What do you think?

Is that cool or what?